The
Château de Résenlieu

LORD BERNERS

The Château de Résenlieu

TURTLE POINT PRESS
AND
HELEN MARX BOOKS

*Design by Wilsted & Taylor
Publishing Services*

Publisher's Cataloging-in-Publication
*Berners, Gerald Hugh Tyrwhitt-Wilson,
Baron, 1883–1950.*
Château de Résenlieu / Lord Berners.
p.   cm.
LCCN 00-130186
ISBN 1-885586-15-9
1. *Berners, Gerald Hugh Tyrwhitt-Wilson, Baron,*
1883–1950—Journeys—France—Normandy.
2. *Novelists, English—20th century—Biography.*
3. *Diplomats—England—Biography.   4. Composers—*
England—Biography.   5. Normandy (France)—
Description and travel.   I. Title.
PR6003.E7425 Z464 2000   823'.912 [B]

Printed in Canada

The
Château de Résenlieu

The
Château de Résenlieu

I left Eton at the end of 1899, and in the spring of
the following year I went to France, as a first step
towards preparing myself for the Diplomatic Service.

In the first years of the Twentieth Century, the diplomatic examinations were a good deal more elemen-
tary than they became later on, foreign languages
being the only subjects that required any very high
degree of technical knowledge; and it was customary
for embryo diplomats, instead of going to the Univer-
sity after leaving their public schools, to embark on
a sort of protracted Grand Tour, spending several
months in France, Germany, Italy or Spain in order to
get a thorough knowledge of the languages of those
countries. In those happy far off cosmopolitan days,
when international war still seemed a remote menace,
and there were no passports, a large number of private establishments on the continent took in young

Englishmen for this purpose. One of these institutions was the Château de Résenlieu in Normandy. It had been strongly recommended to my mother. The Chatelaine, Madame O'Kerrins, was the widow of a French-naturalized Irishman and the daughter of a Comte de Nollent, an impoverished aristocrat who had further impoverished himself by extravagance and unfortunate speculation, so that, when he died, he had little except the Château to leave to his daughter. Monsieur O'Kerrins, who was a scholarly man, had the idea of converting the place into a sort of superior "pension" and after his death Madame O'Kerrins continued to carry on the business alone.

I had never been abroad and my excitement increased as the day for my departure approached. Ever since my childhood there had been shaping itself in my mind an idea of foreign countries that endowed them with something of the enchanted atmosphere of fairyland. Among other delights I believed that I should find there freedom from many things that irked me at home, freedom from parental interference, and above all from the tyranny of games and sport. I had often heard foreigners, and particularly the French, criticized for not being sporting, for frivolity and laxity of morals, all of which deficiencies at that time appealed to me.

My mother announced her intention of accompanying me to France and personally delivering me into the hands of Madame O'Kerrins. I was getting on for seventeen. My school days were over. I considered that I had reached an age when a certain amount of independence was my due and the implication that I could not be trusted to travel alone was a little humiliating. I also foresaw that the journey would not be made easier by the presence of my mother. In matters which lay outside her own particular sphere, which was that of the household and the hunting field, she was curiously inefficient. A railway journey, even in England, was a source of anxiety to her—and also to me, when I travelled with her. It was always attended by muddles and minor catastrophes. I was relieved to hear that her maid, Dawson, was to accompany us. Dawson was the highly competent type of British lady's maid and, although she had never been out of England and had an insular contempt for foreigners, she would, I knew, be capable of coping with any emergency that might arise.

My mother would never admit to any inefficiency on her own part, especially to me, before whom she thought it imperative to keep up the semblance of parental infallibility. She took no advice as to the most convenient mode of reaching our destination. She looked up Résenlieu on the map and decided that the most direct route was via Newhaven and Caen. It was perhaps the most direct route on the map, but it was decidedly the most complicated and uncomfortable. It would have been simpler and quicker to have gone by Paris and one of the shorter channel crossings. However, as I subsequently came to appreciate, my mother's errors of judgement sometimes turned out to be blessings in disguise, and the route she had chosen was by far the most picturesque and romantic method of approach.

At the end of the second week in April we set out. The crossing was by night and it was already dark when we got to Newhaven. The boat we found awaiting us must surely have been the smallest of all the channel steamers. It looked hardly seaworthy. There were no private cabins, only a rather dirty saloon that smelt strongly of food and engine-oil. After my mother and Dawson had settled themselves on bunks in the saloon I went up on deck with the idea of making the most of my first experience of going abroad, but any hopes I may have had of conjuring up an adventurous spirit of eighteenth century travel were frustrated by the growing motion of the boat which, although the sea was what is described in weather reports as "moderate," was beginning to rock and toss about in the most alarming manner. I returned to the saloon where I found my mother and Dawson both sound asleep. There were not too many passengers. All of them were French except for an English clergyman and his wife with whom I was sure that my mother would make friends on the following day, if she had not done so already. The French passengers had a good deal to say to one another and were rather noisy. Particularly voluble were two men in mackintoshes and bowler hats. I was mortified to find that I was unable to understand a single word of what they were saying. After a protest from the clergyman they quieted down, and I was able to get to sleep.

When I awoke next morning a dim light was filtering through the portholes and the boat seemed to be coming to a standstill. Nobody appeared to be getting ready to land and after a short pause the boat moved on again. The steward said it would be another hour before we reached Caen. We had arrived at Ouistreham and were entering the canal which led to Caen. It was enough for me that we had reached the shores of France. I rushed up on deck in time to see the houses of a small sea-port moving silently past in the halflight. With the anxious haste of one who arrives in the theatre just as the play is beginning, I settled myself in the prow of the boat to witness, an enthralled spectator, the lifting of the curtain on France. On both sides of the canal there were long lines of poplars whose reflections on the surface of the water looked like sleepers on a liquid track. Through their slender trunks and the tracery of their branches the landscape began to unfold itself in the growing light. It was not unlike certain parts of southern England. There was nothing very strikingly different, but the sensation of being abroad for the first time in my life, of experiencing at last the reality of this long dreamt-of world, determined by imagination to see something entirely new and marvellous in every aspect and incident of the awakening countryside—a labourer in a blue smock wheeling a barrow of faggots, a woman riding side-saddle on a donkey balanced by a huge basket of vegetables, a group of washerwomen kneeling at the water's edge whacking bundles of linen with wooden clappers. There was a frosty nip in the air and a scent of charcoal and roasting coffee. Overhead the sky lightened to a pale transparent blue and the light mist that lay on the fields began to dissolve in a golden glow. I had not often in the normal course of my life had occasion to appreciate the early hours of the morning. At home I always stayed in bed for as long as I was allowed to do so. At school where I had been obliged to rise early I had not had much time to indulge in the idle contemplation of nature. The novel experience of enjoying the crystalline purity of the day before it became dulled by "the trivial round, the common task," heightened the intensity of my perceptions.

By the time we reached Caen the sun was well above the horizon and the panorama of the town with its steep roofs, towers and churches was bathed in the warm sunshine of a glorious spring morning.

My mother appeared on deck and I saw that, as I had anticipated, she had made friends with the clergyman and his wife. The sight of them talking together I found a little damping. It was not that I was anti-clerically disposed. I felt at that moment that I didn't want an English clergyman and his wife to be mixed up with my first impressions of France, and I was relieved when they said goodbye to us on the landing stage and went off to catch an early train.

Our own train didn't leave until a couple of hours later, and after going through the customs we had breakfast at a little restaurant on the quay. Although I had been brought up in the tradition that to comment on food indicated greed and bad manners, I was unable to conceal my delight in my first French meal, in the omelette, the croissants, the rich Normandy butter partaken of in the open air in a little enclosure outside the Café.

After this, Baedeker in hand, we made a hasty tour of all the starred buildings and churches, but neither the "majestic simplicity" of the Trinité nor the "dignified simplicity" of St. Etienne—the distinctions are Baedeker's—nor the historical associations with William the Conqueror made so vivid an impression on my mind as the mere aspect of the streets, the shops, the people and all the minor features of continental life that differed from those of England, features which because they were new and strange, must have coloured to an exaggerated extent the picture of the whole, for when I revisited Caen again some years later I was unable to find in it any resemblance to the town which had remained in my memory. The things that had so thrilled me in that first rapid and rapturous glimpse had in the meanwhile become commonplace from my having seen them so often elsewhere and they no longer evoked the same emotions, no longer served as landmarks. I was bitterly disappointed. It also happens that the imagination, when excited by some new experience, tends to embroider on memory, adding embellishments that are found wanting when the experience is repeated, and we are seldom able to recapture the mood inspired by our first impressions of a place. It was a mistake to have revisited Caen. I should have left it in the glowing light of my first morning in a foreign town.

My critical sense had been numbed by the novelty of the scene. It was only in the railway station that the patriotic pride which prompts the traveller to exclaim "they order this matter better at home" began to assert itself. Here I was forced to admit that the organisation of travel in France didn't run as smoothly and as respectably as in England. It was marked by an almost amateurish spirit of improvisation and was accompanied by a good deal of shouting and gesticulation. There was a decided lack of official dignity. The station itself had a more squalid appearance than any English station I had seen. The station officials were not impressive figures and the porters were dressed anyhow, some in blue blouses, others in shirt sleeves, and all of them unshaven and begrimed. (A stern look appeared on Dawson's face as though she were about to confront a jacquerie.) At the same time they had a touch of humanity that was lacking in their less emotional English colleagues. It would be advisable, I felt, to establish a personal relationship in order to secure the best of their attention. Being unable to do this through the medium of language I had to recourse to more material methods. Knowing that my mother was inclined to be economical in the matter of tipping, I surreptitiously pressed a few extra francs into our porter's hand. Instead of pocketing the money impassively as an English porter would have done he said "Merci, mon bon petit monsieur" and gave me so beaming a smile that I felt I had made a friend for life.

The French trains were less massively constructed than the English ones and had more the status of a tramcar or an omnibus, an impression that was emphasized when, for the first few hundred yards we passed through the streets of the town in the midst of carts and pedestrians in the most democratic style and I wondered if we were going to continue the journey along roads and country lanes. There was something too of a comic element in our progress. At the level crossings women looking like Mrs. Noah came out of signal boxes, waved a red flag and blew a toy horn. It didn't seem like serious travelling—more like going on a picnic. From beneath the carriages there came a spasmodic banging that sounded as if there were something wrong with the axles. The compartment smelt strongly of inferior tobacco and the seats were upholstered in coarse white lacework which gave it a frivolous, summery look. In the place where in English trains there is usually a mirror there was a small window communicating with the next compartment and my mother, starting to arrange her veil before it, found herself staring into the face of a bearded Frenchman.

I settled myself in a corner seat and observed the scenery. Judging by the succession of views that flitted past the windows I thought the country looked good for painting. When sketching at home I had often found it necessary to cheat, to alter the position and the shapes of trees, to eliminate ugly buildings, to invent foregrounds. Here everything seemed to "compose" naturally, as if arranged by a master of design. In the English landscape there was often a little too much respectability for my romantic taste, too many neat looking fields, too many trim hedgerows and smug looking red brick cottages. The Victorian age lay heavy on the landscape of Constable and Turner and the English countryside often looked as if it had been tidied up by an efficient housemaid. Here in France picturesqueness was rampant. The trees, though less finely grown than English trees, were more graceful in shape, the buildings less neat but more harmonious in form and colour. I was glad that I had secretly packed my paint box and sketching materials and at the moment I thought more of the pleasure I was going to have in painting the country than of the purpose for which I had come to it.

My mother and Dawson had also been examining the scenery, both, I thought, with a slight air of disapproval. After a while Dawson remarked "They don't seem to have such nice cows in France as they do in England." My mother gave a sigh—she was thinking perhaps that it didn't look very good hunting country—and returned to the novel by Mrs. Humphrey Ward that she was reading.

We arrived at Résenlieu shortly before midday. The station, which consisted of a single creeper-clad chalet, was distinctly rural and appeared to have a poultry farm attached to it. Hens encumbered the platform and the railway track and seemed to regard the train as an intrusion, barely getting out of its way and indignantly clucking as it moved on. An antiquated landau awaited us, driven by a coachman in an antiquated livery.

The Château, about a quarter of a mile distant from the station, was pointed out to us by the coachman as we approached it. A half-timbered house of rose-coloured brick with tawny brown shutters on the windows, a steep slate roof and tall chimneys, it stood on the side of a hill surrounded by trees. The facade was overgrown with creepers; all this verdure in and around the house, and the way leading to it through a deep lane overhung with elder bushes, made one think of the Sleeping Beauty's domain. The impression however was dispelled by the Chatelaine who appeared in the doorway as we approached the house. Madame O'Kerrins looked very much awake. She was a tallish woman of ample proportions and was dressed in a flowing peignoire of grey silk. Her white hair, puffed out over her forehead, gave her an eighteenth century look. She reminded me of Madame du Deffand in the portrait by Carmontel but, instead of the sightless eyes, hers were alive and piercing. She had a rather loud authoritative voice and although her manner was at the moment extremely amiable, one felt that it might easily become formidable.

There was a moment of slight embarrassment when

she mistook Dawson, in her black dress and bonnet looking eminently respectable, for my mother. But Dawson, with the subservient dignity of a lady's maid, tactfully established her position by ignoring the proffered hand and attended ostentatiously to the luggage as it was taken off the carriage.

Madame O'Kerrins led us through a panelled hall into a small drawing room which seemed to me, accustomed as I was to comfortable, rather overcrowded Victorian interiors, to be sparsely furnished. The white and gold Louis Seize chairs looked a bit flimsy and an Empire sofa against the wall not very much more substantial. The room had high windows down to the ground opening on to a balcony and the curtains were of striped magenta and cream brocade. The walls were covered with toile de Jouy dotted with vignettes of agricultural scenes and hung with eighteenth century portraits and one or two landscapes in gilt frames. There was a grey marble mantelpiece with a mirror over it and on it, an Empire clock and crystal candelabra. There was an absence of knick-knacks such as I had come to believe necessary to a conventional drawing room, only on a round table in the centre of the room there was a small vase of flowers and some books. Everywhere I noticed signs of change and decay. The stuffs were faded and threadbare, the mirror tarnished, the Aubusson carpet sun-bleached and in places torn. Yet in spite of this air of dilapidation the room was gay and attractive; any impression of bleakness one might have had was precluded by its ancien régime elegance, by a prevailing note of intelligence and taste.

"Your son," Madame O'Kerrins told my mother, "will be quite alone with us for several weeks. Other English pupils will be coming later on. It is lucky for him that it should be so. He will learn our language all the quicker, having no opportunity to speak his own."

After a few polite questions about the journey and my first impressions of France, Madame O'Kerrins took us out on the balcony to admire the view which was certainly very delightful. Immediately in front of the house was a narrow grass terrace, flanked by rose bushes and from it the ground sloped steeply down to a strip of water—*la pièce d'eau* Madame called it, a convenient phrase obviating the term "pond" so offensive to landed proprietors. In the middle of it was a small island planted with chestnuts and larches. The park was bounded by a belt of elms and beyond this the valley widened out into an expanse of pasture land, small fields enclosed low hedges which reminded me a little of the chessboard country in *Alice Through the Looking Glass*. In the far blue distance was a line of wooded hills. The view was extensive but at the same time intimate, and seemed to carry out the general design of the domain. The little town of Gacé, scattered over the opposite slope of the valley to the left, looked as if it had been placed there for an ornamental purpose like the artificial ruins and temples of an eighteenth century park.

I was taken to my room. It was a largish attic-room with beams appearing in unexpected places and a ceiling that followed the contours of the roof. Adjoining it was a powder-closet containing a round tin bath and a rather primitive washhand stand. Not a conventional bedroom judged by English standards, more like a lumber-room. However, it delighted me because its walls were hung with the most brilliant scarlet linen, a stuff, I subsequently learnt, called "andrinople." I had never seen anything like it before, and Madame O'Kerrins was a little surprised by my enthusiastic exclamations. It must, I think, have been the same material as that described by Proust in the sitting-room of Tansonville "of so vivid a scarlet that it would catch fire if a single sun-ray touched it." And indeed when the sun came through my windows in the early morning the whole room would glow like a fiery furnace.

"I hope," my mother said, "that you won't go mad living in this room." I was not disturbed by the idea. Better be mad than dull; and, as my windows looked out on to the view that I had admired from the balcony below, I thought that were I to find myself becoming too excitable I could easily restore my calm by the contemplation of this soothing prospect.

The luncheon hour had been delayed for our benefit—usually the midday meal was at half past twelve. Two more members of the household appeared in the dining room. One was an anaemic looking youth with a black beard whom Madame O'Kerrins introduced as her nephew and addressed as Gerard. He was only a few years older than myself but the black beard created a formidable impression of seniority. The other was a diminutive woman with a tight little face, a swarthy complexion and rather beady eyes. Her dark hair was scraped up into a knot on the top of her head. She was very plainly dressed in a tailor-made costume but a profusion of oriental jewelry, bangles, necklaces, brooches added an exotic touch to an otherwise prim exterior. She looked like a secretary who told fortunes as a sideline. She was a distant relation of Madame O'Kerrins and helped in the administration of the household. Her name was Mademoiselle Laurens but she was always known as "Baghdad." Her father had been Consul in Baghdad and she was born there. Even the servants referred to her as Mademoiselle Baghdad.

There are few things more humiliating than one's first attempts to be amiable in a foreign language. I was dismayed to find that since the days of my Swiss governess I had completely lost the faculty of conversing in French. I felt myself reduced to an almost sub-human level—to that of a dog trying to express its thoughts to a human being. Mademoiselle Baghdad made no move to help out my tentative phrases. My efforts to describe to her the incidents of my journey seemed alternately to puzzle and offend so that I was kept in perpetual fear that an uncertain vocabulary had led me into impropriety.

Gerard, who sat on my other side, was more helpful. He pointed to objects on the table and said "couteau" or "fourchette" or whatever they happened to be. But his method was no less humiliating than Mademoiselle Baghdad's negative attitude. I was unable to explain to him that I knew the words and that it was inability to link them into a sentence that paralyzed my speech, and although he seemed kindly disposed there was an air of martyrdom on his face. I was depressed by the thought that until I could speak a little more fluently I should continue to be a nuisance to all concerned.

The coachman who had driven us from the station waited at luncheon wearing a different livery which also looked as if it had survived from a past generation, a blue tail-coat with silver buttons, a striped red and yellow waistcoat and white cotton gloves. This man, whose name was Gustave, and his wife, Marie, ran the establishment between them. She cooked and looked after Madame O'Kerrins. He was butler, coachman, valet, gardener—he called one in the morning and brought up breakfast and hot water. Later he could be found skating about over the parquet floors with chamois leather pads attached to his feet. He worked in the garden, looked after the poultry and drove Madame out in the landau in the afternoon. There seemed to be no limit to the variety of his functions.

My mother was amazed and a little shocked by his versatility. At Althrey each servant had his or her "place" and would protest "It's not my place" when asked to perform some work of supererogation. "In

England," my mother said, "one could never run a house of this size with only two servants." There was, I thought, a note of pride in her assertion, although she admitted that it would save a good deal of bother if one could—and afterwards she appeared to find consolation in the discovery of deficiencies in the service. The familiarity with which Gustave and Marie treated their mistress would certainly not have suited her, Gustave entering into the conversation at meals and Marie taking a decided line in the kitchen.

I asked Dawson what she thought of backstairs life abroad. "They seem nice people," she said, "and uncommonly civil. But they're a bit funny, sort of independent you know and we had rabbit for dinner."

It was warm and sunny out of doors and we had coffee on the balcony. Gerard went off on his bicycle to Gacé where he worked in a bank, as a preliminary, Madame O'Kerrins told us, to some more important financial position elsewhere. Madame O'Kerrins and Mademoiselle Baghdad retired to their rooms and my mother announced that she was going to write some letters, which was her formula for taking a nap, a habit that, for reasons of physical pride she was unwilling to admit.

Left to my own devices I walked down the grassy

slope to explore the little lake. Spring was well on its way and everything here was more advanced than in England. The limes and the chestnuts were bursting into leaf and cuckoo flowers were beginning to appear in the lengthening grass. The banks of a little stream that ran into the lake were covered with marsh mari-golds. The surface of the lake was still but the reflec-tions of the fleecy clouds that passed across the sky gave it a silent animation. A gentle breeze coming from the direction of the house brought with it a faint aroma of wood fires and roasting coffee—a character-istic scent of France it seemed to me—which mingled delightfully with the fragrance of the spring foliage. An extraordinary feeling of well-being came upon me, such as I did not remember experiencing since the early days of my childhood when I used to wander in the fields at Althrey as yet untrammelled by any sense of discipline or responsibility. The air I breathed seemed full of liberty and lightness. I seemed to have recaptured the innocent childish delight I used to feel in the presence of nature. I stood for a while gazing in ecstasy on the water over which the reflections of the clouds slowly moved.

I knew that I was going to be very happy at Ré-senlieu. I had already taken a great liking to Madame

O'Kerrins and the place enchanted me. There can be "love at first sight" in the matter of houses as in the case of people and, as I looked up at the Château with its creeper-clad facade and its tawny shutters, affection settled in my heart.

I did not feel sorry that my mother was returning to England on the following day. I was looking forward to the enjoyment of complete independence in this new chapter of my life, to the extent of not wanting my mother to have time to become familiar with the ambience in which I was going to live; I didn't want her to have any definite basis on which to advise or control me from afar. I was still very fond of my mother but my love for her was too often disturbed by anxiety as to the form her maternal solicitude might be going to take.

Of this an example occurred that evening after dinner when we were alone with Madame O'Kerrins in the drawing room.

Like many Protestants of her day my mother believed that Roman Catholics were perpetually on the prowl to ensnare innocent Protestant souls. She had never forgotten an incident that occurred in my early childhood. A young lady who was a Roman Catholic came to stay at Althrey. At the age of six I fell deeply in love with her. She seemed to me a paragon of charm and beauty and the fact that she was a Roman Catholic added, in my eyes, an exotic lure to her other attractions. I noticed one day on her dressing table a small necklace of beads which, she told me, was a rosary. Taking it to be some sort of magic talisman connected with her religion I displayed so persistent an interest that she ended by making me a present of it. I thought it wiser not to show it to my mother and for several nights I wore it round my neck under my nightgown, in which position it was discovered one morning by my nurse. I explained to her that it was to keep off evil spirits. "You wicked child," she cried and rushed off with it to my mother who at once concluded that the gift formed part of a design to convert me to the errors of Rome. The young lady whom I loved was not invited to Althrey again.

Subsequently, although I never showed any signs of wishing to change my religion, my mother continued to be obsessed by fears. She suspected that people with artistic temperaments were more likely than others to be attracted by what she called "the theatricalities of Papistry." She would frequently try to intimidate me by invoking family tradition. "If you were ever to become a Roman Catholic," she would say, "your Grandmother would never speak to you again and your father would disown you." There might, I thought, be some advantage in the former contingency. As for my father, I know that he took no interest whatever in my spiritual welfare and would not have cared if I had become a Papist or a Mahommedan.

Now, the prospect of leaving her only son in a Roman Catholic household aroused once more my mother's fears.

"I am sorry to hear," she said to Madame O'Kerrins, "that there is no Protestant church in the neighborhood. I was under the impression that there were quite a number of Protestants in Normandy. I fear that my family may be concerned to hear that my son will have no opportunity to attend Protestant worship. I must tell you that if he were to desert the religion in which he has been brought up it might materially affect his prospects. I hope therefore that it is not too much to ask that you will refrain from discussing religious matters with him."

A twinkle came into Madame's eyes. I guessed that it was not the first time she had had to deal with the religious scruples of parents.

"You may rest assured," she answered, "that neither I nor anyone in this house will make any attempt to unsettle your son's religious convictions. I am not sufficiently fanatical a Catholic to have any wish to proselytize. I have as little desire to convert your son to my religion as I imagine he has to convert me to his."

I found the conversation very embarrassing and tried to disassociate myself from it by turning over the pages of a photograph album on the table. Happily the entry of Mademoiselle Baghdad with the coffee pot put an end to any further discussion. I felt more than ever that my mother had become a greater responsibility to me than I was to her.

As I walked back to Résenlieu on the following morning after seeing her off at the station my mind reverted to leave-takings on similar occasions. I remembered the anguish I had felt when she left me at my private school to face alone the new and alarming conditions of life. At Eton I had seen her go with only a faint regret. Now, my mood was one of intense relief.

Next morning I began my French lessons with Madame O'Kerrins. We worked in a small room adjoining the drawing room. The window looked out on to a clump of lime trees and between the trunks one could see the town of Gacé gleaming in the distance, a charming view which often took my mind off my work.

Madame O'Kerrins's method of teaching was simple and perhaps not very professional, but the charm and humour with which she taught compensated for any lack of professional technique, and inspired me with a desire to do her credit as a pupil. She used to give me an article from the *Figaro* or a passage from some classical work to translate into English. I would then translate it back into French and my version would be compared with the original.

In the matter of conversation she advised me to go ahead without at first paying too much attention to grammar. "Grammatical correctness," she said, "would come with practice. Don't be afraid of making mistakes and of being laughed at. The Englishman's national pride is apt to make him cautious and afraid of making a fool of himself. Remember that it is more important for you to learn French than to preserve your dignity."

This, I thought, was excellent advice and I took it. After a couple of weeks I had more than recaptured the fluency with which I had been able to converse with my governess in the schoolroom.

The barrier constituted by a foreign language is like the varnish in an old picture which obscures details of form and colour. Some pictures when cleaned prove disappointing. Such was the case both with Gerard and Mademoiselle Baghdad, and when I became able to speak with them and understand what they said I found that they were far less interesting than I had at first believed them to be.

The atmosphere of mystery that had seemed to surround Mademoiselle Baghdad was merely the effect of her oriental jewelry, her swarthy complexion and the romantic character of her birthplace. She was in reality a very ordinary type of little old maid. The imagined background of the Arabian Nights was reduced to that of a French provincial town. She was in fact a little like a foreign version of my cousin Emily, a purely negative character. She was bigoted and disapproved of almost everything. Luckily she was without cousin Emily's malevolence and her militant manners. She had no interest that I could discover. She was inefficient even in household matters. "One can never rely on Baghdad," Madame O'Kerrins would say, "for any practical assistance."

I wondered why Madame O'Kerrins had her to live with her at the Château and came to the conclusion that she found it necessary to have somebody at hand with whom she could find fault. Mademoiselle Baghdad's role in the household was that of a "souffre-douleur."

The emergence of Gerard's character was even more disappointing. The early impression that his beard made upon me—that he was a man of the world, vastly superior to me in the wisdom born of experience—was completely dispelled and he turned out to be an extremely foolish young man, foolish to the point of being almost half-witted. I suspected that his impressive beard merely concealed a receding chin. There was no subject on which he was capable of expressing a sensible opinion. He knew nothing of art, politics or even sport. He never read a book or newspaper. His only redeeming feature was a sort of flaccid amiability. Madame O'Kerrins did not seem to care for him very much and scarcely appeared to notice him. His presence was only due to family feeling. He was the son of a sister of whom she was fond.

If these two members of her household were a little lacking in interest, the deficiency was amply made up for by Madame O'Kerrins herself. The more I came to know and understand her the more my admiration for her increased. She was a very remarkable woman and it seemed to me that her capacities were wasted in teaching young Englishmen French in a remote country house. She should, I thought, be presiding over a salon in Paris, if such things still existed. I had read a certain amount about French social life in the eighteenth century and I came to the conclusion that it was not only in physiognomy that she resembled Madame du Deffand. She had the same rather formidable personality tempered by the same kind of wit and charm. She was inclined to be intolerant of facile enthusiasm and excessive earnestness. Her attitude to the times in which she lived was one of contemptuous aloofness. She disliked the Republic—"Cette grosse Marianne," she used to say, "Chaque jour elle devient plus vulgaire"—and she disliked President Loubet for being President of the Republic. Also for being in favour of the revision of the Dreyfus case. Madame O'Kerrins was violently anti-Dreyfusard. The case which was very much on the tapis at that time was one of the few subjects that caused her to lose her habitual calm and good humour. When President Loubet's top hat was bashed in at the Auteuil Races by an anti-Dreyfusard she was delighted. The incident seemed to give her renewed hopes for the future of France.

In conversation she would sometimes indulge in a mild Voltairean blasphemy, but she went regularly to Mass and was on the best of terms with the Curé whom she frequently invited to the house. Ceremonial religion represented for her no doubt one of the last links with the etiquette of court and it was in keeping with her eighteenth century personality to have a tame Abbé about the place. She was apt to be a little slovenly in her clothes. She would come down in the morning in a not over-clean peignoire and her beautiful white hair was often untidy. However these defects

were redeemed by her aristocratic appearance and the dignity of her carriage, just as the shabbiness of the furniture in the house was less noticeable on account of the taste with which it was arranged and the prevailing air of distinction.

My working hours were limited to about three hours in the day. The rest of the time I was able to devote to the Arts without fear of reproof or interference. As soon as my mother had left I took out my paint box and sketchbook. There were plenty of subjects in the immediate neighbourhood of the house and I didn't have to go very far to find them. I was a born "plein-airiste." Painting in the open air brought a sense of concentrated joy that I never felt when painting indoors.

The other day while investigating a long unexplored cupboard I came upon a volume of watercolour drawings that I had made of Résenlieu at that time. They were not very good but they brought back to me, more forcibly than any diary could have done, the mood of exhilaration in which they had been painted.

The transition from spring to summer that year in Normandy was one of singular lushness and brilliance. This impressed me all the more vividly as for several years I had lacked the freedom and leisure to enjoy this particular season. At school, even at Eton, there were too many incidents of school routine to occupy my mind and distract me from the observation of natural beauty. Although time had a little faded the colours of these sketches there was still evidence in them that the spring had gone to my head and that I had used the most daring greens and yellows that I could find in my paint box in order to do justice to the tones of the grass and the foliage. Looking through the sketchbook I was able to recapture even the physical sensations of the moment, the freshness of the breeze on my face, the heaviness of thunder in the air, an obtrusive ray of sunshine that dried too quickly my "washes," the scent of a syringa bush nearby, the croaking of frogs seeming to deride a failure—a study of foliage reflected in the water which I attempted many times without success.

When it rained and I was unable to paint out of doors I used to retire to the library where there was a piano, an aged Erard, that had belonged to Madame O'Kerrins's mother. It was a little the worse for wear but it had a pleasant mellow tone and a key-touch so light that even the most elaborate runs were easy to play.

It is often difficult, especially when one is young and ideals of felicity are uncertain, to know when one is being really happy. The life I was now leading at Résenlieu left me in no doubt. It was the kind of life I had often dreamt of but had never hoped to realise so soon.

The happiness I had enjoyed at home or at school had nearly always been mingled with an alloy of parental interference or of school discipline. Nobody at Résenlieu seemed to think it unnatural that I should wish to spend my time in painting or playing the piano. It was delightful to feel that I could follow my inclinations without incurring disapproval or contempt, that I was no longer expected to be earnest about things that didn't interest me. It was exhilarating to wake up every morning in the knowledge that there lay before me a day of freedom and independence in the course of which no too strenuous form of work or play was going to be forced upon me.

At home I had always found getting up in the morning a rather painful process. Here it was one of the most agreeable moments of the day. At eight o'clock Gustave brought me my breakfast which consisted of café au lait and croissants (those delicious crescent shaped rolls half bread half pastry) with butter and confiture, a breakfast considerably less substantial than that to which I was accustomed at home. However, for the pleasure of having it in bed I felt that I could willingly forego the eggs and bacon, the sausages, the kidneys, the English coffee for which one had to hurry down to the dining room where more often than not there prevailed an atmosphere of gloom. The English are seldom at their best at breakfast time and when they are it is even more depressing.

Through the open window there floated in to me as I lay in bed the scents and sounds of the country, the aromatic odour of the creepers covering the house, the twittering of swallows in the eaves, the distant cackling of poultry, the lowing of cattle. On fine mornings when the sun, striking through the eastern window, lit up the scarlet hangings of my room filling it with a fiery glow that seemed an augury of excitement and joy, I would be roused to a sudden energy and springing from my bed I would rush out of doors in search of subjects to paint in the afternoon.

One of the principal charms of the Château, it seemed to me, was that it was so very much in the country, far more so than any other country house I had hitherto lived in. At Althrey, at Arley, one was in less immediate contact with nature which was kept at bay by well-mown lawns, gravel paths, neat clipped hedges and garden walls. Here at Résenlieu nature surged up to the very doors. The creepers that came in at the windows, the unkemptness of the garden, the weeds on the drive (that had so distressed my mother), the untrimmed hedges, the general air of neglect seemed to vaunt the triumph of nature over domestic organisation. Even Gustave working in the garden, his livery exchanged for a peasant's blue blouse, seemed in league with nature, for his labours never made the garden any tidier.

Soon after my arrival I had learnt that there was a fourth member of the household who had not yet appeared. This was a young lady bearing the pleasantly sounding name of Henriette de Malherbe, a niece of Madame O'Kerrins, who was confined to her room by illness and would not, I was told, be able to come downstairs for a week or so. Her presence, Madame O'Kerrins implied, would bring a livelier note to the company than that supplied by Gerard and Mademoiselle Baghdad. All that I had heard about this young lady in the conversational allusion and some photographs I saw of her in an album aroused in me a violent interest and a glimpse I caught of her in her window as I was standing in the garden was as encouraging as the portrait of the princess sent in advance to the suitors in the fairy tale. I worked myself up into so high a state of suspense that when she finally did appear I was a little disappointed.

But my disappointment was only momentary. Mademoiselle Henriette's looks were of a kind that depend on cumulative effect and have to be observed in every variety of mood before they can be fully appreciated. She had a mobile face and sometimes even looked plain. But the vivacity and the intelligence of her expression gave her face a greater attraction than could have been achieved by a more static beauty. Taken separately her features were not particularly good; her nose a little too retroussé; her eyes a little on the small side; her lips a little too full. But the general effect of her face was charming. She had a delightful dimpled smile and her eyes were curiously light grey and had the luminosity of moonstones. Her hair was light brown and according to the fashion of the day was puffed out at the back and gathered into a knot on the top of her head. She was simply and not particularly fashionably dressed. Her style was picturesque rather than "chic," a better model for a painter than for a modiste. She had a good figure, a little plump perhaps but it was the plumpness of youth and would fine down as she grew older—she was not more than seventeen or eighteen. She had a natural grace and an instinctive sense of what suited her and I noticed that whenever she put on a hat or a shawl casually without looking in the mirror she always did so in a way that most became her.

From the first words exchanged with Mademoiselle Henriette I foresaw that we were going to like one another. There was an immediate easy sense of affinity that precludes the necessity for any very laborious process of making friends. Attraction was strengthened by the discovery of similar tastes. Mademoiselle Henriette liked music and painting without knowing enough about either subject to be unduly critical, always a satisfactory condition for an amateur enthusiast—and an equally favourable basis for friendship was provided by the fact that her opinions about the other inmates of the Château coincided with my own. She adored Madame O'Kerrins, she had a rather mocking affection for Mademoiselle Baghdad and Gerard she found ridiculous and tiresome. She teased Mademoiselle Baghdad and made fun of her and treated Gerard with such contemptuous aloofness that I was often quite sorry for him—but at the same time rather pleased.

Madame O'Kerrins had been right. Henriette did certainly bring an element of gaiety into our midst. I had been contented enough with life at the Château as it was, with my admiration for Madame O'Kerrins, with the pleasure the place itself and my artistic occupations afforded me—even with the company of Mademoiselle Baghdad and Gerard who, although they contributed little, were at least unobtrusive. Now with the addition of Henriette my happiness was complete.

Under the influence of French surroundings my artistic ideals were transformed. I no longer hankered after Turneresque scenery. Romantic visions of Swiss mountain passes and lakes, the castles of the Rhine shimmering in iridescent mist were now displaced by the more definite forms and colours of the Normandy landscape. I transferred my allegiance from Turner to the Barbizon School. In the library I discovered some volumes of an art journal containing reproductions of the pictures of Corot, Rousseau, Daubigny. In the drawing room there was a small picture by Harpignies

of a green valley with a stream and a line of tall poplars.
These pictures became my guiding stars. I was as yet
unacquainted with Sisley and Monet. I should like to
be able to say that I discovered Impressionism off my
own bat, but the impressionist effects that appeared in
my sketches were due to incompetence rather than to
any deliberate method.

My musical taste was similarly affected. It was no
longer dominated by Wagner. His music seemed to me
now too Teutonically grandiloquent, Wotan, Fricka,
the Valkyries too heavy-footed on the Aubusson car-
pets and amongst the delicate eighteenth century
furniture. There was perhaps also a mute protest in
the air, memories of 1870 when German officers had
been billeted in the house. In addition, both Madame
O'Kerrins and Henriette were not enthusiastic about
Wagner. "Comme c'est Allemand," Madame O'Kerrins would exclaim when I played his music to her.

I returned once more to my former love Chopin,
and in the Nocturnes, the Mazurkas, the Impromptus
I found a note of tender sentimentality more in har-
mony with the place and my present mood, and with
the preferences of the ladies of the house. As I played
to them after dinner in the library by candle light I
thought of Chopin playing to George Sand or to the
Misses Sterling.

The library at Résenlieu had an atmosphere of melancholy charm. It seemed to be used chiefly as a repository for things that their owners had not had the heart to throw away. Dilapidated chairs of different styles, a large capitonné sofa of the Louis Philippe period with the stuffing coming out in places, tables covered with broken knick-knacks, empty bonbonnières and off volumes of the *Revue Hebdomadaire*. In one of the windows there stood an elaborate contrivance of wire for holding flower pots with a couple of dead geraniums in it. The only feature of the room that was in contrast to the general air of neglect was the parquet floor which was always kept highly polished and shone like a mirror.

The room was long and narrow. It had five high windows on one side and a glass door at one end with steps leading down into the garden. The curtains were of faded green silk and the pelmets intricate with folds and tassels. The bookshelves with their gilt and russet volumes reached up to the ceiling. Trees grew close up to the windows and their foliage filled the room with a soft green light which on hot summer afternoons created an impression of leafy coolness and seclusion.

No one ever came into the room during the daytime and I was able to read or play the piano there undisturbed. It was the room I preferred to all others. Half of its charm consisted in its shabbiness and I would not have had it otherwise. In the hotch-potch of time-stricken furniture there was not a single piece that was actually offensive and one could trace in it a history of selections inspired by discrimination and taste.

Taste, that was the keynote of the house, a sense of elegance to which comfort was often sacrificed. There were no sofas or armchairs on which one could sprawl or lounge. The Louis Seize chairs in the drawing room were more agreeable to the eye than to the posterior and had been designed, one might think, to enforce an alertness of posture in an age when it would have been considered a breach of good manners to relax either physically or mentally. Even in these less ceremonious times one hesitated to do so in the drawing room at Résenlieu and the conversation that took place there required a certain alertness of mind. It was very different from the sort of conversation I was accustomed to at home, with its slovenly phraseology, clipped words and unfinished sentences. However trivial the subject might be, it had style and even the trite observations of Gerard and of Mademoiselle Baghdad seemed to have an epigrammatic quality.

I had been a little startled at first by the freedom with which the natural functions of the body were discussed. In England such things were taboo. Laxatives were advertised cautiously; in chemists' shops ladies would wait until they were alone before asking for a pill and one could always cause embarrassment by mentioning the water-closet. "Je me suis purgé ce matin," the Curé announced one day at luncheon. The information was received without comment and I thought of the consternation that would have been caused at Althrey by such an admission on the part of Mr. Bassett.

Another thing that surprised me was the way in which food was discussed in France. In the England of those days it would have been considered as ill-bred to embark on a technical discussion of food as to exalt some lady's intimate physical charms or to speak of God in theological terms. The average Englishman didn't very much care how his food tasted as long as it was of good quality and he got plenty of it. Victorian Puritanism condemned the glutton less severely than the epicure and thought it less sinful to over-eat than to devote attention to rendering more appetising what was eaten.

At home and at Arley meals had been copious rather than interesting, while at school they had been frankly unpalatable. I had not had much opportunity to appreciate nuances in the methods of preparing food. Strawberries and cream and roast pheasant were my highest ideals in the food line. At Résenlieu the seeds of a more subtle Epicureanism were sown and I began to interest myself in questions as to whether tarragon were preferable to chervil in a sauce or as to the number of times the potatoes should be removed from the foaming butter and allowed to cool before being served, and I used sometimes to go into the kitchen with Henriette to watch dishes being prepared without feeling that I was making a nuisance of myself or incurring the stigma of greediness.

There was something in Gerard's manner that for a while continued to puzzle me. As a general rule he was obsequious, even humble and I can say without being unduly conceited that he was in most things inferior to me. He was stupider, uglier, less popular with ladies and even his tennis was worse than mine. Nevertheless I couldn't help noticing that in his bearing towards me there was a mysterious note of patronage and that he held a slightly contemptuous opinion of young Englishmen in general. At last I discovered that it was due to a feeling of superiority in the matter of sex.

"It is true is it not," he said to me one day, "that most Englishmen remain virgins until they marry?"

I said that I didn't believe that this was so.

"But yes," he insisted, "friends who have been in England tell me."

"I don't know what opportunities your friends had to investigate the matter," I said, "Englishmen as a rule don't talk very much about such things."

"Ah," cried Gerard, "it is because they have nothing to talk about. The young Englishmen they have no temperament. They do not think about women."

"They think more about games," I said, "and hunting and shooting."

"Le sport," exclaimed Gerard contemptuously. "In England it is nothing but le sport. The English are a nation of schoolboys. In France we are more serious."

I felt that there was something wrong about this. I had been brought up in the belief that the French were decidedly more frivolous than the English. I had no desire to argue about the relative merits of sport and sex. However, Gerard seemed determined not to abandon a ground on which he felt he was scoring.

"You have no bordels in England," he went on.

I was not sure and replied that anyhow there were plenty of tarts on the streets.

He became personal. "You yourself, you have been with women?"

I was bound to confess that I had not.

"You are now how old?"

"Sixteen and a half," I replied.

"Ah," he cried with an air of triumph, "at sixteen I had already been with many women. And now," he added, "I have here in Gacé a mistress, a very charming mistress, a married woman."

Having delivered this knock-out blow he was inclined to be magnanimous. "You shall see her," he went on, "I shall take you to her house one day and I shall present you."

"That will be very kind of you," I murmured.

"Yes, I shall present you to her. But of course, you must not say a word of this to my aunt."

"But surely she wouldn't mind," I said.

"She wouldn't mind, no, but she is not discreet. The husband is a jealous man and it would be terrible for my poor Emma if his suspicions were aroused."

Her name, he told me, was Emma Jouvet. She was the wife of a doctor in Gacé. Henceforth, whenever I was left alone with Gerard, he would launch out into the most extravagant praise of his mistress. He would tell me how beautiful she was, how chic, and above all how passionate. I asked if she was as attractive as Henriette. He snapped his fingers angrily. "Henriette," he exclaimed. "Mais Henriette n'est rien a coté. Du reste Henriette n'est qu'une petite gamine mal elevée."

My curiosity to see this paragon was aroused and when Gerard informed me that the absence of Madame Jouvet's husband favoured an opportunity for the promised visit I readily gave up an afternoon of sketching in order to accompany him to Gacé.

We set out in a spirit of rather self-conscious secrecy as if on an amateur smuggling adventure. In the outskirts of the town Gerard stopped before an unpretentious little house with a brass plate proclaiming it the residence of "Docteur Jouvet, Medecin." The door was opened by a young woman of plain and respectable appearance whom at first I took to be a maidservant. It was not until Gerard pointed to her proudly and said, "Voilà Emma," that I realized that this was Madame Jouvet herself, Gerard's much vaunted mistress. It seemed impossible that this drab looking little woman could be the person whose charms and passionate nature had been so dithyrambically extolled.

I disguised as best I could my surprise and disappointment. What had amazed me even more than Madame Jouvet's unprepossessing appearance had been her air of respectability. There was nothing about her that suggested the glamour of illicit love. Her figure was rather dumpy, her face as devoid of animation as a biscuit and of rather the same colour. Her get-up and the way in which her hair was dressed did nothing to relieve the uncompromising insipidity of her features.

Madame Jouvet showed us into a small drawing room on the first floor and motioned us to be seated as formally as if we had come for a consultation with her husband. The room was stiflingly hot. The blinds were down, the windows tightly shut and the curtains drawn. An odour of mildewed stuffiness mingled with the effluvium of cabbage and lavatory that filled the rest of the house. In the semi-obscurity I could see some modern Louis Quinze chairs upholstered in mustard coloured rep, little constellations of plates on the walls, a standard lamp with a fly blown flounce, a palm with its pot wrapped in crinkly pink paper, over the mantelpiece an enlarged photograph of a bald middle-aged man with pince-nez, presumably the Doctor.

As we sat making desultory conversation I was assailed by an intolerable sense of depression and claustrophobia. Madame Jouvet offered me a glass of tepid syrupy grenadine which, to relieve my embarrassment, I gulped down. Happily unconscious of my reactions to his love-nest, Gerard assumed an air of proprietary complacence. He sat down beside Madame Jouvet and attempted to fondle her. She cast an anxious glance in my direction and pushed him away whispering, "Mais non, Gerard, tu es fou."

The moment had come, I thought, tactfully to leave them to their amours. I got up, but Gerard cried out, "Stay, one is so well here." He thought no doubt that I had not had time to appreciate the bliss of having a mistress. Madame Jouvet pressed on me another glass of grenadine. My discomfiture was growing acute. At last, feeling that I might at any moment be sick, I jumped to my feet and took so rapid and decided a leave of Madame Jouvet that I was out of the room before Gerard could stop me. He followed me down the passage. I explained to him that I felt faint. "She is charming is she not," he said. "Absolutely delightful," I assured him. "Ah," he said, kissing his hand to the air, "you can have no idea how that woman is passionate."

It had been a terrible experience and one that might well have had a serious effect on the trend of my sexual life. Incidentally it spoilt for me my subsequent reading of *Madame Bovary.* I was never able to disassociate Emma Bovary from the drab little doctor's wife in Gacé.

I loyally kept my promise and spoke to no one of Gerard's liaison. However, I found that my silence had been unnecessary as the whole of Gacé knew about it, and the doctor himself, far from being jealous, was in the habit of boasting of his wife's *affaire* with an *homme du monde.*

The little town of Gacé which looked so inviting seen in the distance scattered over the hillside proved disappointing as soon as one got inside it. An insignificant provincial town unmentioned in Baedeker, it was totally lacking in any kind of charm or individuality. The houses had a "close fisted *cossu* middle-class air" and looked as if they were inhabited by notaries and prosperous retired tradesmen, as in fact they were. The castle dominating the town with its massive round tower and pointed roof looked impressive from afar but was in reality devoid of any architectural interest. The church situated on the edge of the town made a picturesque feature in the distant view but near at hand it was seen to be of modern construction and the interior was a horrible specimen of ecclesiastical vulgarity.

I disliked going into the town and never went there unless it was absolutely necessary, for it was there that I discovered for the first time that the English were not popular in France. The Boer War, I gathered, was the principal reason for this hatred of England. The subject was carefully avoided at the Château but in the streets of Gacé the less reputable members of the population were liable to shout "Vivent les Boers" at me as I passed and on the walls of a public lavatory I saw scrawled up the words "A bas l'Angleterre." I was dismayed by these manifestations of hostility towards my country for which I desired popularity as much as I did for myself. In my ignorance of international politics, lulled by the complacent atmosphere of Victorian England, I had imagined that the Parliament of Man, the Federation of the World was on the eve of being realised and it came as a shock to me to find that nations could still hate one another. I had believed that all that sort of thing was over now except of course in the case of people like the Boers or the Zulus who misbehaved themselves and were impertinent to the British Empire.

Madame O'Kerrins did not have much intercourse with the inhabitants of Gacé. There was one old lady who visited the Château fairly frequently. Her name was Madame Bonnet and she lived in a large, ugly house near the church. In her garden there grew the largest begonias I had ever seen. Madame Bonnet told me that their size and their beauty were due to their being manured by the corpses of cats. In the bedding

out season she used to offer a small reward to anyone who brought her a dead cat and when a sufficient
number had been collected they were used as a foun-
dation for the begonia beds. It seemed to me a rather
macabre idea and I thought that at night the garden
must be haunted by the ghosts of cats miaowing and
caterwauling. These flowers were in a way symbolical
of Madame Bonnet herself. The widow of a former
Préfet, she was well off and enjoyed a certain consid-
eration in the town. Like Anatole France's Dame The-
roulde "comme elle était riche on la disait de bonne
renommée." She was always dressed in black and her
garments had an expensive, slightly official air as be-
fitted the widow of a Préfet. She had a somewhat des-
iccated appearance but her face, in curious contrast,
was round and full, and curiously well preserved for
her age which was between sixty and seventy. Her
greyish hair was arranged with a virginal simplicity.
Her expression was one of great sweetness. She gave
the impression of having been permanently saddened
by the wickedness of the world. In the sweetest, gen-
tlest of tones she would recount the most hair-raising
tales about the misdeeds of her neighbours. Every
time she came to the Château she would serve up
some horribly scandalous piece of gossip with the air

of one offering an innocent gift of flowers or fruit. She would invariably present it with a preamble of pious commiseration for the person concerned. "Poor Madame X. It is terrible what they are saying about her. I can't think how people can be so wicked and malicious. They say that she has immoral relations with her own sons, such nice boys and so young, only sixteen and seventeen. Of course there's not a word of truth in it." She would then proceed to reel off a list of incriminating facts accompanied by details so vivid and convincing that one was left in no doubt as to the truth of the accusations. She would then sigh heavily and sometimes even a tear would glisten in her eye.

At first I was completely taken in by Madame Bonnet and was quite surprised when Madame O'Kerrins remarked one day that Madame Bonnet was one of the nastiest, wickedest old women she had ever known. "That mask of charitable long-suffering," she said, "conceals a boundless energy of hatred and malice."

Madame Bonnet was supposed to write anonymous letters but she had never been caught out. The only authenticated charges that could be brought against her were that she had foreclosed on a mortgage thereby reducing some of her late husband's relations to penury and that she had so tormented a maidservant in her employ that the girl had been driven to suicide. However, in the latter case Madame Bonnet seemed to have behaved very well in face of the *fait accompli* and laid some of her choicest begonias on the unfortunate girl's coffin.

I asked Madame O'Kerrins why, holding the views she did about Madame Bonnet, she saw so much of her. She said that she couldn't help being fascinated by so perfect a specimen of triumphant hypocrisy. In her social tastes Madame O'Kerrins was something of an entomologist and Madame Bonnet certainly was a specimen.

In an educational magazine (called, I think *Je Sais Tout*) I read an article on the Praying Mantis and, as it contained a number of technical phrases, I used it in the course of my lessons for purposes of translation. When I read to Madame O'Kerrins the description of this insect "with its horrible knife-edged forelimbs folded in a devotional attitude as if to deceive unwary victims with a semblance of piety," she said, "C'est Madame Bonnet."

Two other specimens of Madame O'Kerrins's collections were Monsieur and Madame de Rosen, an elderly couple who for the summer months rented a pretty little house on the confines of the Résenlieu estate.

Monsieur de Rosen looked like a superannuated beau of the Louis Philippe period. He had smooth, rather long grey hair brushed back from his forehead, a bulbous nose and a drooping moustache which at intervals he would blow away from his mouth, a gesture that gave him the appearance of an angry walrus. He always wore a grey frock coat, a buff coloured waistcoat, a panama hat and carried a pair of white kid gloves and a gold knobbed cane.

I imagined at first from his accent and his deportment that he was of German origin, but it appeared that he was Polish. He would sometimes expatiate on the grandeur of his lineage. A king was even mentioned, Jean Sobieski, if I remember aright. He was supposed to be a composer, but I was never able to discover what he had composed. Madame O'Kerrins thought he had written an opera that had been performed in Warsaw. At all events he never spoke of his own works nor did he deign to play them on the piano. I gathered that he considered it beneath his dignity to publish anything and expose himself to the impertinence of critics. His opera, perhaps, had been a failure. "Music," he said, "is essentially a personal, a private art." I objected that if all composers held that opinion we should have very little music. "It would be as well," he said. He seemed to have taken an embittered view of music in general and there were few composers he allowed to possess any merit. Beethoven, Bach he admitted, and Chopin, presumably for patriotic reasons. For all modern composers he had the greatest contempt. He had a particular dislike of Wagner and said that a single bar of Chopin was worth all Wagner's works together. He ws not encouraging about my own piano playing. He told me that my technique was entirely incorrect and that, if I wished to take up the piano seriously, I should have to start all over again from the very beginning.

It was true that my style of piano playing was amateurish. As piano lessons had been denied me I had been obliged to evolve a method of my own. My performance had more temperament than accuracy. However, I had a good musical sense that enabled me to "get away with it" and impress people who didn't know very much about piano technique. Madame O'Kerrins and Henriette enjoyed my playing and were even more annoyed than I was by Monsieur de Rosen's criticism.

Madame de Rosen was of a singularly massive

build. She was rather short but she made up in width for what she lacked in height. She resembled a perambulating mountain and as she had white hair and dressed always in white, Henriette had nicknamed her "Mont Blanc." Monsieur de Rosen had intimated confidentially that his wife was inclined to be exacting in the matter of conjugal duties and Madame O'Kerrins said one day "Poor man. He is obliged to make the ascension three times a week and finds it very exhausting."

Madame de Rosen's enormous face reminded one of a pantomime head and was very heavily rouged and powdered. The summer heat had a disastrous effect on her make-up and on very hot afternoons there would occur a sort of spate of cosmetics. Often, on arriving at the Château, she was obliged to retire to Madame O'Kerrins's bedroom to repair the ravages of the inundations.

Two or three times a week the de Rosens used to come up to the Château in the afternoon to play whist with Madame O'Kerrins, Mademoiselle Baghdad or the Curé making a fourth. It always amused me to watch them from the balcony coming up the steep path that led to the house, Monsieur de Rosen prancing ahead, continually stopping and looking round impatiently at his wife, like a dog out for a walk with a slow-moving mistress. Nothing would induce her to hurry. She seemed to have confidence in her bulk and one felt that she would have moved with deliberation even out of a burning house.

The de Rosens were a strange couple. They were devoted to one another and had been so for some forty years, yet there seemed to exist between them a perpetual state of nervous tension. This was most apparent when one or the other was talking. They were both very loquacious and while Madame held forth Monsieur would hum to himself and tap on the table. When Monsieur monopolized the conversation, Madame would close her eyes and sigh aggressively. They both had the irritating conjugal trick of correcting one another's assertions.

They also belonged to the category of people who may be termed "unfortunate" in the true sense of the word. They seemed to attract minor mishaps, generally of a comic nature. The Deus Ridiculus, the Harlequin God had them as victims for his slapstick ministrations. If Gustave upset the sauce-boat it was sure to be over Madame de Rosen's white dress. If there were a hole in the carpet Monsieur de Rosen would inevitably catch his foot in it, and once, after a game of whist, Mademoiselle Baghdad inadvertently pulled his chair away as he was about to sit down so that he sat heavily on the floor. If they came with us on one of the weekly picnics they would be bound to sit on a wasp's nest or tread in a cow-pat.

The picnics at Résenlieu had been for many years a sort of weekly institution. I am not sure if Madame O'Kerrins really enjoyed them, but she thought that the English did, and looked upon them as a suitable entertainment for her English pupils. I am bound to say that the Résenlieu picnics were pleasanter than such diversions usually are and, except when the de Rosens brought with them their knockabout element, they were not attended by the contretemps and minor disasters that as a rule accompany picnics.

The neighbourhood abounded in favourable spots for a *déjeuner sur l'herbe*, flowery banks by the river-side, mossy glades in shady woods, the ruins of a cas-tle, a friendly farm house where a table would be set for us in the courtyard. Madame O'Kerrins drove in the landau taking with her the luncheon baskets and the de Rosens when they came, while the rest of us bi-cycled or walked. The food was always delicious, pâ-

tés, galettes, flans, vin du pays, cider, coffee or choco-
late heated up over a spirit lamp. As soon as the meal
was over I would rush off to paint, thus avoiding the
nuisance of cleaning the dishes and packing up. In any
case it seemed in France to be the duty of the younger
ladies of the party to attend such matters. I remember
once in a neighbouring house when I attempted to as-
sist in handing round the coffee, the hostess said to me
with an air of surprise "Mais Monsieur vous faites la
jeune fille."

In my early adolescence I was always anxious to do the
right thing. I knew that any manifestation of eccen-
tricity was considered to be "in bad taste," whether it
consisted in wearing brown boots on Sunday or in
disliking cricket or fox-hunting. School and family
life had taught me the necessity of concealing any
lurking tendency to be different from other people, the necessity of conforming. I believed that, in
France, an amorous adventure, an *affaire de coeur* was
thought as important as, in England, the pursuit of
manly sports, that if a young man thrown into the company of a young and attractive girl did not promptly
fall in love with her he would be accounted a poor
creature indeed.

Thus it came about that I fell in love with Henriette. If there was some degree of self-conscious effort in the summoning up of my passion, it was helped by the season and the environment, by the soft summer climate, the fragrance of flowers that filled the air as if with the incense of love so that I came to experience all the usual symptoms of love's fever. Henriette's voice, her laughter, her movements, her changes of expression filled me with exquisite delight. I was thrilled anew each time she came into the room. When I thought of her in her absence, as I was out walking alone or as I lay awake at night, my heart glowed with a wild exaltation.

However, in spite of these violent emotions it was a case of "*si jeunesse savait*" and my love was innocent and chaste, unsullied by physical lust, rather a muffish affair in fact. My raw-youthful awkwardness and timidity curbed even the temptation to gaze at her too ardently, so that the object of my passion remained unaware of the vehemence of my feelings, which, after all, were a little like those aroused by a work of art in a gallery which could be admired and worshipped but never made one's own. I knew in the light of reason that nothing could ever come of this one-sided love affair, that it was part of the magic atmosphere of Résenlieu, delightful, transient and unreal as a dream. That was, no doubt, why I was not prostrated by anguish and horror when Madame O'Kerrins happened to mention that Henriette was engaged to be married. I only felt hurt because Henriette had not told me herself. I was a little indignant with her for having led me on, which was unreasonable as the poor girl had done nothing of the sort, having, as I have said, been unaware that I had felt anything beyond pleasure in her company.

I pressed Madame O'Kerrins for further information about her niece's engagement.

"A good match," she said, "for Henriette who has no 'dot' to speak of."

"Is she very much in love with her fiancé?" I enquired.

"She has not seen very much of him," she replied. "It is what we call a '*mariage de convenance*.'"

I suppose I must have looked rather glum for she went on: "The idea does not please you? You find it unromantic?"

"At first sight," I said, "it doesn't appear very romantic. But perhaps the young man is attractive."

"Not very," said Madame O'Kerrins, "and he is not particularly young. But he is quite well off. Such marriages are often more successful than love matches. *L'amour passe, mais l'argent reste.* At least that is what one hopes. He is a steady fellow and not given to extravagance or injudicious speculation. *Il sera cocu peutêtres. Voilà tout.*"

These matter of fact views about marriage were, I thought, characteristic of Madame O'Kerrins, but I found them echoed by Henriette when I reproached her for not having told me of her engagement.

"I didn't tell you about it," she said, "because I didn't think it would interest you. It is not very interesting."

"I should have thought that marriage was a fairly important event in a girl's life."

"Important, yes, but not necessarily interesting. One doesn't want to be left stranded like poor Baghdad so it's just as well to take an opportunity when it comes, provided of course, that it isn't too repulsive. At the worst marriage can always be a stepping-stone to higher things."

She didn't actually quote Tennyson, but that was the sense of her words. Although I was inclined in those days to be impressed by cynicism—I had a kind of snobbish admiration for it—I was a little shocked by such cynical views coming from a young lady for whom I had entertained a sentimental regard and she lost in my eyes some of her romantic glamour. I had less difficulty in reconciling myself to the hopelessness of my passion. I was no Werther, and my relationship with Henriette settled down to a condition of emotion remembered in tranquility.

Life at Résenlieu continued to flow on calmly and delightfully. Nothing very exciting ever happened but there was in the air a perpetual simmering of pleasant activity. The days that passed were like the pages of a diary of trivial events kept by someone with an intense *joie de vivre.*

It was during this halcyon period that I became aware of curious moods of exaltation that would sometimes come upon me, attacks of ecstasy almost orgiastic in their violence.

I can remember the first time this experience occurred. I was standing one night at my bedroom window looking out at the nocturnal landscape as I had often done before. The countryside was bathed in soft moonlight. Down below, in the shadow of the trees, the lake gleamed faintly and the frogs were croaking passionately as they always did on hot summer nights. Apart from this there was silence and immobility.

Everything in the house was still. Outside no wind stirred the leaves. The circumstances of that evening were not noticeably different from those of any other. Nothing had happened to stimulate my mind or to bring me any special happiness. All at once my tranquil enjoyment seemed to swell to a greater intenseness, my senses to be endowed with a magical receptive capacity. It was as if the scene before me, the silvery radiance of the sky, the deep, velvety shadows of the woods, the gleaming surface of the lake, were about to reveal some rapturous significance, some glorious reality hitherto concealed from my normal vision. How long this ecstasy lasted I know not. Time was in abeyance, the ephemeral character of human life was illusory. I was only conscious of an immeasurable passionate delight. If I had had the religious gift I should have no doubt believed it to be some form of divine revelation of which faith would have supplied the meaning. As it was, although it passed away and seemed to leave everything as it had been before, there remained a feeling of encouragement as if from a premonition of some eternal and wonderful reality lying behind the appearance of things.

Another time a similar kind of ecstasy came upon me in the course of a morning walk. My lesson with

Madame O'Kerrins had been postponed and, as I didn't feel inclined to paint at the moment, I set off for a ramble along the narrow lane at the entrance to the drive which led up the hill to a stretch of moorland, where the landscape so horribly resembled a picture by MacWhirter* that, on reaching the spot on previous occasions, I had turned back and gone no further. This time, braving the depressing effect this bit of scenery habitually made on me, I went on across the moorland to where there was a descent into the valley on the further side. Passing through a little wood of beech and Spanish chestnut (The MacWhirter effect was over), I found myself in a deserted quarry, overgrown with brambles and flowering shrubs. In a corner of the quarry, against a low cliff of yellow stone overshadowed by hawthorne and elder bushes, a pool had formed. At the water's edge there was a broad strip of velvety moss. The place teemed with insect and animal life. Glittering dragon-flies hovered over the water and across its surface water boatmen

* *Note.* MacWhirter was a Royal Academician whose pictures were very popular at the time. There was one at Arley purchased by my uncle Luke. Photogravures of his work are said to be found in lodging houses and provincial hotels.

skimmed. Frogs croaked unseen, water-newts disported themselves and lizards scurried through the tufts of grass or basked among the pebbles in the sunshine. There was a warm aromatic scent in the air and the scene was dappled with alternate patches of sunlight and shade. On the bank above the cliff a pair of hoopoes appeared flaunting their striped orange and russet plumage and their gay crests. It was as if a vignette out of Gilbert White's *Selborne* had come to life and all my childish passion for natural history revived once more. I remained for a while in contemplation of the scene, oblivious of time, and when finally I tore myself away from it the magic impression of the place continued to colour my thoughts as I walked home.

I spoke to Henriette of my discovery with such wild enthusiasm that she looked a little surprised, as though confronted by one who "on honey dew had fed and drunk the milk of Paradise." As soon as luncheon was over I insisted on her coming with me to see it. "Well really," she exclaimed, "to drag me all this way to look at this silly old stone-pit."

And indeed now the magic of the place was gone. The dragon-flies still flitted over the pool, the lizards scurried among the pebbles, the hoopoes were there, the sun shone as brightly as it had shone that morning

and the shadows were as deep. In all its details the natural appearance of the place was the same, but it no
longer seemed "apparelled in celestial light." Its glory
had passed away.

Perhaps, like the landscape-garden in Headlong
Hall, its charm depended on the character of unex-
pectedness ("Pray Sir," said Mr. Milestone, "by what
name do you distinguish this character when a person
walks round the grounds for the second time?"), or
more likely it had been a private vision incommunica-
ble to others. I often visited the spot again in the hopes
of recapturing once more the enchantment of that
first impression but never was I able to do so.

The happiness I was experiencing at Résenlieu had
the effect of making me live entirely in the present. I
rarely gave a thought to the diplomatic examination
or to my future career. Memories of home and Eton
faded. Even Deniston, with whom I fancied I had
formed a lifelong attachment, seemed now to belong
to a closed chapter in my life. I had written to him soon
after my arrival at Résenlieu giving him what I had believed to be a vivid account of my favourable impressions of the house and its inhabitants. He had written
back, "You seem to have struck rather a dull place.
Why don't you go to Paris?" I was alienated by what

seemed to me a lack of sympathetic understanding. Surely, I thought, he should have realised that life in a French country house and intimacy with such people as Madame O'Kerrins and Henriette represented a far more suitable form of enjoyment than Paris visited in the circumstances of any British tourist. I didn't write to him again.

My only link with home was my correspondence with my mother and this I looked upon as something of a corvée. My letters to her were wanting in either inspiration or spontaneity. It was necessary to exercise the utmost caution to avoid telling her anything that she might seize upon as a motive for alarms and excursions. The slightest provocation would elicit expressions of maternal anxiety. "I hope you are not getting into a foreign way of thinking." "I hope you are not falling in love with the niece." This sort of thing infuriated me, seeming as it did to drag me back into the nursery, and made me almost dread the eventual return to England and the interferences of home life.

Towards the end of July Gerard left. He was going to Paris to pursue his financial career in more elevated circumstances. During his last days at Résenlieu he became intolerable, assuming the air of patronizing contempt for the Château and its inhabitants, harping on the joy he felt at escaping from provincial surroundings to the metropolis where he was going to find a more suitable scope for his talents and activities. I asked him if he felt no regret at leaving behind his beloved Madame Jouvet. "Poor woman," he said fatuously, "she already belongs to the past." Madame O'Kerrins took all this in a spirit of amused sarcasm. "We shall no doubt," she said, "have reason to be proud of our Parisian nephew. I hope you'll not forget your poor old country aunt in the midst of your successes." "I shall write. I shall write," Gerard assured her graciously. "Don't break too many hearts," Henriette implored him.

My mother, whom I had told of the departure of the only other male member of the household wrote, "I don't like the idea of your being left alone with nothing but female society." I was able to reassure her that I was shortly to have the company of three compatriots. Madame O'Kerrins had told me that three young Englishmen were coming to Résenlieu at the beginning of August. Their names were Battersby, Carver and Essington. Battersby, she said, had been at Eton. The name conveyed nothing to me and I concluded that he must have been one of the obscurer members of the school.

I was a little apprehensive of this invasion of what I had come to look upon as my private paradise. I feared the possibility of my losing the priority I enjoyed in the affections of Madame O'Kerrins and Henriette. I had of course the advantage over them of being an habitué. On the other hand they were three against one. When they arrived I was relieved to find that there existed no particular bond of union between them beyond the convenience of travelling together. And I soon discovered that my fears of my ascendancy being disputed were groundless. Madame O'Kerrins and Henriette discussed the newcomers with me as if I were a member of the family.

Battersby, the Etonian, was decidedly the least attractive of the three boys. Eton had given him a veneer of man-of-the-world that only made his shortcomings less excusable. He was short, stocky and heavy in appearance. His face had the congested, aggressive expression of an angry goose. Dullness and ignorance did not prevent him (it seldom does) from being argumentative. With a firm grasp of the wrong end of the stick he would belabour subjects to death. He was a prodigious bore. Even Mademoiselle Baghdad, who put up with most people in a spirit of long-suffering toleration, would occasionally sigh and mutter in an aside, "Mon Dieu, comme il est assommant, ce monsieur!"

In addition to this I discovered that he was obsessed by a chronic sense of grievance. He was forever complaining that he had not been given some athletic distinction or other at Eton, that there was a tendency to pass him over in favour of people often of inferior merit. I felt that there was something about him that would inevitably excite the desire to withhold rewards from him even when they were his due. I thought of what my father had once said to me. "Always mistrust a man with a grievance."

He had a dreadful sense of humour that consisted in the retailing of anecdotes culled, one suspected, from *Everybody's Book of Jokes,* anecdotes that generally began with the formula "A Scotchman, an Irishman and a Jew," ending with one of the nationalities scoring off the other two, the kind of jokes that appear on the backs of a certain modern brand of matchboxes.

Carver had been at Harrow but my loyalty to Eton didn't prevent me from liking him a good deal better than I liked Battersby. He had a rather agreeable pug-face that wore an eternal grin. He also had a sense of humour but it was a good deal more spontaneous than Battersby's, so spontaneous in fact that it often became embarrassing. This was his first experience of a foreign country and everything about the French, their customs, their clothes, their language seemed to strike him as excruciatingly funny. He was continually going off into such paroxysms of mirth that Madame O'Kerrins thought at first that he was not quite right in his head.

While Battersby was stupid Carver was silly, which is not the same thing and infinitely more disarming.

Of the three I liked Carver best but Essington was the most interesting. I had come across types like Battersby and Carver but Essington was something strange and new. He was rather effeminate looking, the kind of boy who is nicknamed Molly or Nelly by his schoolfellows. But he had never been to school and had been privately educated. He had fair hair, a pink and white complexion, a slightly receding chin, and large blue eyes that gazed appealingly at nothing in particular. He was always beautifully dressed—a little too beautifully sometimes—and his shirts and ties were of the most exquisite pastel shades. A rather languid aloofness gave him the air of a privately printed edition de luxe.

He was the son of *nouveau riche* parents. His mother lived apart from his father, a fact of which Essington seemed a little proud. He disliked his father "who, you know," he once confided to me, "is just a teeny bit vulgar." Mrs. Essington, without being of the fashionable world, had fashionable aspirations which she seemed to prefer to indulge on the continent, in foreign capitals, on the Riviera or in fashionable foreign watering-places. Essington spent a good deal of his time abroad in the company of his mother and a tutor. I gathered that Essington's father, who was a rather tough business man, had a pretty poor opinion of his son and was not very much disturbed by his preference for his mother. Essington had acquired an ultra-sophisticated continental facade which at first impressed me. I soon discovered, however, that there was nothing much behind this facade and that the interest he expressed with regard to aesthetic matters was superficial and fashionably frivolous. In music he liked Chaminade and Louis Ganne, the composer of a mazurka much in vogue at the time called "La Czarina" and the "Marche Lorraine," while the literature he preferred was the *Vie Parisienne* and the novels of Gyp—not that I have anything against either *La Vie Parisienne* or Gyp (whom Nietzsche admired) but as the high spot of anyone's reading they seemed to me a little inadequate.

I had also the impression that Essington spoke French very well—he certainly spoke with a tremendous French accent—but when I said to Madame O'Kerrins that I wondered if I should ever be able to speak French as well as Essington she replied, "Indeed I hope you never will," and went on to say that his accent was ridiculous, that he had no notion of grammar and that his vocabulary gave the impression of having been picked up in Riviera hotels. "Il faut dire," she added, "que je le trouve un tout petit peu rasta." *

Neither Battersby, Carver nor I were in the least suspicious of Essington. We attributed his "queerness" to the fact that he had not been to Eton or Harrow. The only time he really shocked us was when he mentioned Oscar Wilde one day in quite an unconcerned manner and said that his mother had actually met him.

Those of the present generation can hardly realize the horror Oscar Wilde's name inspired in polite Victorian circles—non inter Christianos nominandum—

---

* *Note.* Rasta is an abbreviation of "rastaquouere," a person of flashy, slightly vulgar smartness.

a horror that persisted even into the Edwardian period. I remember that when I told my mother, à propos of Richard Strauss's *Salome*, that it was based on a play by Oscar Wilde, she exclaimed, "Oh hush dear." The subject of homosexuality was also one that was strictly taboo in those days. By many it was hardly believed in, and I was told that some people when informed of what Wilde "had actually done" declared that such a thing was not possible. I, who had been to a public school, knew that it was, but for a long time I imagined that it was a form of vice that was confined to public schools and only very rarely practised by adults and then only by foreigners.

The tenor of my life at Résenlieu was naturally a little affected by the presence of my compatriots. It lost its remote, idyllic quality and took on something of the atmosphere of school. The attractions of France had to a certain extent weakened my attachment for home and country, but now the companionship of English boys of my own age tended to revive it and I found myself thinking with increased tenderness of Althrey, of Eton and Deniston. Although I remained as devoted as ever to Madame O'Kerrins and Henriette I grew a little more conscious of the barriers constituted by the difference of nationality and language.

There were more picnics and expeditions than before and the evenings were more lively with round games and occasional charades. These latter were performed before an audience of two, Madame O'Kerrins and Mademoiselle Baghdad, who were the only ones who didn't insist on taking part in every charade. Carver showed a remarkable talent for acting, Battersby and Essington none at all. However Essington made up for his lack of talent by devising the most elaborate costumes for himself and taking a very long time in making up his face which rather hung up proceedings.

One evening we had a spiritualistic séance. Mademoiselle Baghdad refused to take part in it on religious grounds, and retired to bed. Later in the evening we revenged ourselves on her by writing astral messages on pieces of toilet paper and shoving them under her bedroom door which offended her virginal susceptibilities and caused her to sulk for several days.

That August was exceptionally hot, and nearly every afternoon we used to go down to bathe in the river Touques, in a bend that formed a spacious pool where the water was deep and still. It was a delightful spot. On one bank there was a line of poplars, on the other a clump of willows overhanging the pool with a strip of turf going down to the water where one could lie in the shade. The flat expanse of flower-spangled meadows beyond the poplars, punctuated by symmetrical groups of trees, was a little like the background of a picture by Puvis de Chavanne, a painter to whom I took an early dislike. However, with the exception perhaps of Essington, there were no anaemically graceful figures floating about in it and, like many things in nature such as sunsets and flower gardens, it was more charming in reality than in artistic reproduction. Of these bathing expeditions I retain ecstatic memories, of the air quivering in the summer heat, the silvery luminosity of the sky and the joy of lying naked on the grass thinking of nothing.

One afternoon as we were returning from bathing we met a funeral on the road, a peasant funeral, simple and pathetic. The faces of some of the followers were distraught with grief as in Flemish pictures of the Crucifixion.

Essington passed by with averted gaze and a slightly contemptuous expression, as if so poor and common a ceremony were unworthy of his attention. I was afraid that Carver, for whom anything met with abroad was potentially mirth-provoking, might be going to laugh. However he contented himself with remarking, "How dull to be dead on a day like this." I noticed that Battersby seemed to be plunged in the deepest gloom and hardly spoke during the rest of the day.

That evening he came into my room as I was going to bed. I feared that he was going to speak to me of some new grievance that had been weighing on his mind or perhaps tell me one of his funny stories. He sat down heavily and after a while said, "Are you afraid of death?"

"Not particularly," I replied, "I try to ignore it."

"So do I. But I can't help thinking about it sometimes. Especially if one is reminded of it by a funeral or something. I know I shan't sleep a wink tonight."

"But why should you be afraid?" I asked. "Don't you believe in God and the future life and all that sort of thing?"

"Of course I do. But all the same the idea of death terrifies me."

"Are you afraid of going to Hell?"

"No, of course not," he replied. "That's to say," he added, thinking perhaps that he had spoken too complacently, "there's no reason why I should. I say my prayers regularly."

"Then I don't see what you've got to be afraid of."

"Well it's just the idea of death, you know. It absolutely terrifies me."

This little glimpse into Battersby's private thoughts

rather disturbed me. I wondered if he were not perhaps more psychologically interesting than he appeared on the surface. I went to bed with the resolve
that I would try and like him a little more. But on the
following day, there he was as usual, with his grievance, his anecdotes about Scotchmen and Jews, his
general state of aggressive obtuseness.

However, the episode had started me thinking
about death. I began to wonder what other people
thought about it. Although I had no very great hopes
of getting anything illuminating from Carver on the
subject, I approached it by saying to him, "You know
Battersby tells me that he is terrified by death."

"And so he ought to be," he replied.

"Why? Do you think he's bound for Hell?"

"No, I expect he'll go to Heaven all right, but some-
how I don't think God'll like him. It'll be like a fellow
who's got into the Sixth Form and whom the Head-
master hates."

Essington showed an even greater detachment.
"Oh my dear," he said, "don't speak to me of death."

I found that at Résenlieu death was not a subject
that people seemed to want to talk about. Madame
O'Kerrins changed the subject at once, Henriette
laughed and asked me if I wasn't feeling well and I felt
it useless to consult Mademoiselle Baghdad. As a big-

oted Papist she would have some cut and dried doctrine about it that would get me no further.

I remembered once discussing the subject with Marston at Eton. He quoted someone as having said that we were all condemned to death with an indefinite reprieve. "I must say," he added, "I should be very annoyed if I thought anyone was going to get off. But as we know they aren't, to me it's quite a consolation."

The time was approaching for me to return to England. It was settled that I should go back via Paris. This entailed spending a night there and crossing over on the following morning. My mother didn't wish me to spend the night alone in a hotel and wrote to ask Madame O'Kerrins if she had any friends or relations in Paris who would be willing to put me up. Madame O'Kerrins said that there was a relation of hers, a Madame Sylvestre, who had a house in the Rue du Bac. "But," she warned me, "Madame Sylvestre is a very old lady and it will be very quiet. However," she added with a smile, "that is no doubt what your mother would prefer."

My brief visit to the Rue du Bac—I arrived at six o'clock in the afternoon and left early the next morning—was hardly typical of what the average English youth might expect of his first visit to Paris.

Madame Sylvestre was, as Madame O'Kerrins had

said, a very old lady. She must, I suppose, have been some fifteen years older than Madame O'Kerrins to whom she referred as "la petite," a singularly inappropriate description, I thought, in view of Madame O'Kerrins's massive, stately figure and her dominant personality. The house had a wonderfully "old world" appearance. The rooms looked as if they had been left untouched since the days of Louis Philippe. There was a very old dog, called Castor. The dining room was a long panelled room at the back of the house, running its entire length and opening on to a garden with an unkempt lawn overgrown with trees. The final touch to the general air of antiquity of the place was supplied by Madame Sylvestre's husband, of whose existence I had been unaware until we sat down to dinner. I noticed that a third place had been laid and, as soon as the first course was served, a door opened at the far end of the room and Monsieur Sylvestre appeared, shuffling very slowly towards the dinner table. I was about to jump up but Madame Sylvestre laid her hand on my arm and said, "Pay no attention to him until he gets quite close. He prefers it so." Monsieur Sylvestre looked well over a hundred. His face was a mass of wrinkles and resembled leather upholstery that had suffered the wear and tear of centuries. He had a long white moustache and he wore a brown velvet scull-cap. His eyes, sunken and colourless, occasionally flashed a glance of ill-temper. He was an alarming looking old gentleman and must, I thought, have been a tartar in his day. But now Madame Sylvestre seemed to have got the upper hand. When I attempted to address a polite remark to him, she said, "It is useless. He is stone deaf."

The old man ate heartily. Age and decrepitude did not seem to interfere with his appetite. I found the proximity of this greedy, totally deaf and rather fierce old gentleman a little embarrassing. When I endeavoured to ease the situation by handing him something I thought he wanted, he shook his head angrily and grunted. Conversation was carried on between Madame Sylvestre, the maidservant, myself and the dog who added to my embarrassment by sitting under my chair and emitting the most appalling smells.

I had seen a good many old people but never before had I come across so concentrated a manifestation of old.

After dinner Madame Sylvestre gave me a latchkey and said, with what I imagine intended to be a wink, "I've no doubt you would like to go out and amuse yourself." It was all very well, but the prospect of

"amusing myself" alone, inexperienced, in an un-
known city, were a little bleak and her words inspired
me with a faint, self-conscious shame. Most of my
contemporaries, I felt, Deniston, certainly Essington,
would have known where to go and what to do. Madame O'Kerrins had suggested my calling on Gerard
but, remembering the visit to Madame Jouvet, I
feared that I might be let in for something similar in
the way of entertainment. My only resource was to go
for a walk and try to get some sort of impression of
Paris.

I crossed the river into the Place de la Concorde ad-
miring its impressive expanse, the obelisk and the
monuments of the French towns. I noticed two in-
scriptions, one defiant, on the statue of Strasbourg,
"La France quand même." The other ironical, on the
wall of the Tuileries Gardens, "Liberté, Egalité, Fra-
ternité. Defensé d'uriner ici."

I stood for a few minutes at the entrance to the Rue
Royale, looking at the brilliantly lighted street, at the
far famed Maxim's across the road, but alas! I had neither the money, the experience nor the proper clothes
to enjoy the pleasures such places offered. Feeling
rather like the Little Match-girl in Hans Andersen's
tale, I made my way toward the dark, romantic look-

ing boskage of the Champs Elysées, looking in, as I passed, at the doors of the Hôtel Crillon, thinking how wonderful it must be to be staying in such a luxurious, expensive looking place.

Ever since, one evening at Eton, I made the acquaintance of a prostitute under the shadow of trees illuminated by a street lamp—an early landmark in the history of my sophistication—lamp-lit foliage in a town had continued to be curiously associated in my mind with vice in its most mysterious and alluring form. As I walked in the shadow of the trees through the alleys of the Champs Elysées, my licentious imagination was aroused to the highest pitch. Couples sitting on the benches, solitary figures wandering in the semi-obscurity, even groups of respectable bourgeois, discussing no doubt politics or domestic affairs, were for me the most intriguing representatives of evil. I longed for adventure. At the same time I knew that if anything of the kind had occurred I should have been terrified. My yearnings were frustrated by the sense of my inexperience. I continued to walk on in a state of almost feverish agitation until at last fatigue overcame me and compelled me to return, unsatisfied and feeling a little foolish, to the Rue du Bac.

From a practical point of view the evening had been

a ridiculous failure, but considered emotionally it had been almost as exciting, and considerably less expensive, than if I had spent it at Maxim's or in a brothel—and in an odd way I had absorbed something of the atmosphere of Paris that continued, for some time after, to feed pleasantly my imagination. Such was my first experience of Parisian night-life.